Goalkeeper

 Clive Gifford

W
FRANKLIN WATTS
LONDON • SYDNEY

NORFOLK
LIBRARIES & INFORMATION SERVICE

1125711	
PETERS	26-Feb-08
796.33	£11.99

First published in 2006 by
Franklin Watts
338 Euston Road
London NW1 3BH

Franklin Watts Australia
Level 17/207 Kent Street
Sydney NSW 2015

© 2006 Franklin Watts

Editor: Adrian Cole
Art Director: Jonathan Hair
Design: Matthew Lilly
Cover and design concept: Peter Scoulding

Photograph credits:
Maurice McDonald/PA/Topham: 19. Empics: 22.
Empics/Topfoto: cover, 4, 6, 8, 9, 10, 11, 13, 16, 20, 21,
23, 24, 25, 27. David Klein/ProSport/Topfoto: 26.
PA/Topham: 3, 7, 12, 14, 15, 17, 18.

Every attempt has been made to clear copyright. Should there
be any inadvertent omission please apply to the publisher
for rectification.

A CIP catalogue record for this book is
available from the British Library.

Dewey classification: 796.334'26

ISBN: 978 0 7496 6509 8

Printed in China

Franklin Watts is a division
of Hachette Children's
Books, an Hachette
Livre UK company.

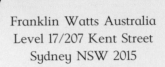

Contents

The greatest game

Football is the most popular team sport on the planet. Every team has a goalkeeper. A goalkeeper's job sounds simple – to stop the other side scoring goals.

▷ HALL OF FAME

Italian goalkeeper Gianluigi Buffon has played over 50 times for his country. In 2001, he became the most expensive keeper ever when he was sold by his club Parma for an amazing £32.6 million. He now plays for Juventus.

△ Gianluigi Buffon dives low to his right to make a fantastic save.

Aim of the game

Football is an exciting game played by two teams. A full match is played over two halves of 45 minutes. The referee is in charge of a game and is helped by two assistants. The aim of the game is to score goals. The team with the most goals wins.

> **Sometimes the goalkeeper, who is often less in the spotlight than his team-mates, can become the hero. And when that happens, it's a great feeling.**
>
> – Alex Stepney, former Manchester United goalkeeper

Peter Schmeichel was a brilliant goalkeeper for Manchester United and Denmark. He won the European Championship in 1992 and the Champions League in 1999 (pictured).

Eleven-a-side

Each side starts a game with 10 outfield players who are defenders, midfielders or strikers. They are joined by one very special player, the goalkeeper. Goalkeepers have to be good gymnasts. They leap high or dive low to make great saves. They also have to be brave to dive at the feet of an opponent.

> **The biggest thing when you are young is to enjoy yourself. After all, what is better than diving around in six inches of mud?**
>
> – Mervyn Day, former West Ham goalkeeper

What is a goalkeeper?

Goalkeepers stand apart from their team-mates. They need special skills and have to follow special rules.

> Keepers suffer less from the physical point of view and don't have recovery problems, which means [their careers are] longer.
>
> – Dino Zoff, Italian World Cup winning goalkeeper

A clean sheet

Goalkeepers are usually the last players who can prevent a goal. They stop the ball by making a save. If they do not let a goal in during a game they are said to have kept a clean sheet.

HALL OF FAME

Dino Zoff was rejected as a teenager by Inter Milan and Juventus. Yet he went on to become a great goalkeeper and captain of Italy. In 1982, he became the oldest winner of the World Cup at the age of 40.

△
Bente Nordby of Norway holds the ball after making a save. She can choose to kick or throw the ball out towards one of her team-mates.

▷ Catching the ball safely from a cross. Goalkeepers must be strong and be able to react quickly, especially when their opponents are trying to score.

Different rules

The goalkeeper is the only player allowed to catch, punch and handle the ball. Goalkeepers can only do this inside their penalty area, a large box marked out on the pitch in front of the goal. Goalkeepers wear a different colour top to their team-mates. Most also wear special gloves that give them extra grip.

> " What kind of a goalkeeper is the one who is not tormented by the goal he has allowed? He must be tormented! "
>
> – Lev Yashin, former Russian international goalkeeper

Part of a team

Goalkeepers are in charge of organising a team's defence. They have to stay alert because they may have to make a save at any time.

> If you are a defender there's nothing better than looking round and seeing a goalie behind you who's in complete control of his area.
>
> – Gordon Strachan, Scottish player and manager

Confidence and anticipation

Goalkeepers need to be confident in everything they do, from taking a goal kick to catching the ball. Experienced goalkeepers become good at working out what may happen next. This is called anticipation. They adjust their position and may run out to clear the ball or jump up to catch a cross before it reaches an opponent.

△ Tine Cederkvist of Denmark watches the game closely. She may have to make a save at any moment.

Communication

Goalkeepers have a good view of the game. They can see how an opposition attack is building up. They may also spot opponents who are in space on their own. If these players get the ball they may have a good chance to score. Goalkeepers let their team-mates know what they see and warn their team-mates so they can defend well.

> Another really important part of being a goalkeeper is communication. It's vital to practise this on the training ground, without the noise of the crowd.
>
> – David James, England goalkeeper

▷ Italian goalkeeper Carla Brunozzi directs her team-mates to form a defensive wall (see page 25).

SKILLS TIPS

• Always watch the game and stay aware of the other team's attacks.
• When giving instructions to your defenders, make them simple and clear and shout them out loudly.
• Watch team-mates in training so you learn how they play.

Fitness focus

Goalkeepers do not run around the pitch as much as their team-mates. Yet, they still need to be very fit and quick to react, so they train and practise very hard.

> " A champion is someone who does not settle for that day's practice, that day's competition, that day's performance. They are always striving to be better. "
>
> – Briana Scurry, US women's team goalkeeper

▽ Fabien Barthez reacts quickly to kick the ball clear of his penalty area.

Train to gain

Goalkeepers work on their general fitness with a range of exercises. They also perform fast footwork drills, such as short sprints, to improve their speed off their goal line. A lot of their general fitness training is carried out with the rest of their team.

▷ **HALL OF FAME**

Goalkeeper Fabien Barthez won both the World Cup in 1998 and the Euro 2000 competition with France.

Injuries and comebacks

Sometimes goalkeepers are injured during the game. They can also get injured in training. Injured goalkeepers have to work hard to get fit again. They aim to keep their body flexible and look forward to the next chance they get to play.

▽ Antti Niemi is taken off the pitch on a stretcher. He was replaced with the team's substitute goalkeeper.

> " Goalkeepers today do some running and work really, really hard. They do a lot of physical work in the week. "
>
> – Chris Woods, former England goalkeeper, and now coach

The backpass rule

Goalkeepers also take part in passing and kicking drills. They have to be able to kick and pass a rolling ball well because of the backpass rule. This stops a keeper from picking the ball up if it has been passed back by a team-mate. Instead, they must kick or head the ball clear.

Training apart

Goalkeepers have a range of different skills that other players do not need. They have to practise these often so they are ready for the match.

> **"** My aim is to become as complete a goalkeeper as possible. For me this means: I have to get better in all aspects. **"**
>
> – Timo Hildebrand, German goalkeeper

Keeping flexible

Goalkeepers need their bodies to be very flexible so they can twist, dive and reach high and low. They use weights to build up their back muscles. They perform a long series of stretches to their body's muscles before training or playing matches.

△ Roy Carroll practises diving at full stretch during a training session.

"I do weights to retain my muscle strength and on the pitch, I do a lot of ball handling. Part of this is catching at least 300 balls a day and also doing a load of diving and twisting."

– Dave Beasant, former goalkeeper

Repeat exercises

Goalkeepers perform long, repeated exercises to help their movement when handling the ball. They may ball juggle with team-mates or throw a ball over their shoulder and twist round to collect it. They practise catching shots hit at all different heights and angles.

△ Goalkeeping coach, Ray Clemence helps England goalkeepers Paul Robinson (left) and David James practise their ball-control skills.

Goalkeeping coaches

A squad's two or three goalkeepers work together. They are usually coached by an experienced ex-goalkeeper who understands the demands of their job. A goalkeeping coach can help correct goalkeeping mistakes and can talk and listen to goalkeepers to help build their confidence.

Positioning

Spectacular saves may impress the fans, but many more goals are stopped by goalkeepers using their brains and feet to get into a good position.

▷

Bente Nordby moves across her goal. She keeps in a good stance, with her body ready for action and her eyes on the ball.

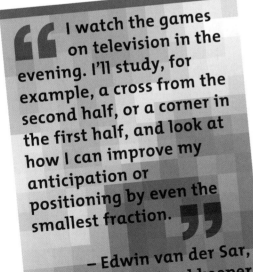

" I watch the games on television in the evening. I'll study, for example, a cross from the second half, or a corner in the first half, and look at how I can improve my anticipation or positioning by even the smallest fraction. "

— Edwin van der Sar, Holland keeper

Stance and balance

For the basic stance, goalkeepers stand with their legs shoulder-width apart, knees bent and hands facing outwards. They are balanced and ready to move in any direction. They may have to rush out of the goal to kick a ball clear, leap and catch a high ball or dive to the ground.

In line

When the ball comes towards a goalkeeper, he or she gets in line with it. This makes it easier to reach the ball if there is a shot at goal. It also allows goalkeepers to move between the ball and the goal. Their body acts like a second barrier, should their hands fumble the ball.

SKILLS TIPS

• Concentrate on the game. You may be called into action suddenly.
• Practise getting into your goalkeeping stance and moving around your penalty area quickly.
• Be aware of where the goal is behind you when you come off your goal line.

One-on-one

A one-on-one situation happens when an attacker has the ball and has only to beat the goalkeeper to score a goal. The goalkeeper often comes out of the goal, but stays in line with the ball. This gives the attacker less of the goal to aim at.

Shay Given times his low dive at the feet of Ryan Giggs. He aims to collect or deflect the ball away from Giggs without fouling him.

> **It is hard sometimes when you don't touch the ball for 20 minutes. You just have to be ready. Wherever the ball moves I move in line with the ball.**
>
> – England women's goalkeeper, Rachel Brown

Handling the ball

The most important skills a goalkeeper learns are how to catch and handle the ball. Goalkeepers always watch the ball as they catch it. They try to catch the ball in front of their body.

It's okay diving around, but you must be confident about catching the ball. You have to believe in your own hands.

– Dave Beasant, former England goalkeeper

◁ Paul Robinson catches the ball safely during an England training session.

High and low

Goalkeepers deal with shots at all heights and angles. They move their feet to get in line with the ball and prepare to punch or catch the ball. When a ball rolls along the ground, goalkeepers drop to one knee. They move their body and other leg behind the ball to act as a barrier.

18

"" Diving does take courage and confidence...You have to time your dive, often in a split second, and concentrate on the ball all the time. ""

– Gordon Banks, former England goalkeeper

▽ This goalkeeper leaps to catch a high ball. He aims to catch the ball at its highest point with both hands spread around the ball.

Diving

When goalkeepers cannot get their body behind a ball they can make a diving save. They take a step in the ball's direction then spring off the foot nearest the ball. If they can catch the ball, they grasp it tightly. They try to land on their side with their body relaxed as they hit the ground.

SKILLS TIPS

• Keep your hands and fingers relaxed so they cushion the impact of the ball as it arrives.
• As soon as the ball is caught, gather it in to protect it.
• If you cannot catch or use your hands to reach the ball, try to get your body, legs or arms up and in line to block the ball.

Cushioning and gathering

Goalkeepers spread their hands around the back and sides of the ball. They catch it and cushion the force so they do not fumble it. After catching the ball, they try to gather it into their body quickly. They wrap their arms around the ball to protect it.

Making decisions

Goalkeepers have to make important decisions during a game. These decisions may affect whether the game is a win, loss or draw for their team.

❝ You have to assume that your defense will be penetrated, and it's at those moments when your actions alone may determine the difference between a win or loss. ❞

– Claudio Taffarel, Brazilian World Cup winning goalkeeper

△ Francesco Toldo comes out quickly to force Hagi into a lob shot which does not score.

Stay or go?

When an opponent has the ball close to goal goalkeepers can stay on or near their goal line, or rush out. If they come out, they must get the angle of their run right. This gives the opponent less of the goal to shoot at.

Catch or not?

Goalkeepers try to catch the ball whenever they can. But sometimes, they may feel they cannot get their hands around the ball safely. They can punch the ball away or try to deflect it around the goal posts or over the crossbar to prevent a goal.

> " I see keepers who punch the ball away towards the middle of the pitch when they could easily catch. I see others who turn it round for a corner rather than keep the ball in play. The reason is simple: many keepers are afraid of making a mistake. "
>
> – Dino Zoff, Italian World Cup winning goalkeeper

▷ Briana Scurry of the USA stretches to punch the ball clear of a crowd of players. She focuses only on the ball, and not on the players around her.

▷ SKILLS TIPS

- When punching, try to punch firmly at the middle of the ball with both hands forming a fist.
- When throwing the ball out, make sure your arm points in the direction of your target.
- Practise your kicking from hand, and your throws too. Try to make them as accurate as possible.

Kick or throw?

Once the goalkeeper has the ball, he or she has six seconds to release it. A goalkeeper can kick the ball, start an attack with a quick, long overarm throw or roll the ball out underarm to a team-mate.

21

Dealing with pressure

Goalkeepers are under a lot of pressure. They are expected to make good saves and no mistakes. However, all goalkeepers make mistakes. Their secret is to be strong enough to forget about them and get on with the game.

> You have to realise that mistakes will happen and they will be highlighted...The important thing is that you bounce back and get on with your job.
>
> – Dean Kiely, international goalkeeper

South Korea goalkeeper Kim Jung-Mi makes a great save under pressure from a crowd of players.

Whoops!

When a striker misses a good chance, the crowd may groan but soon forget about it. But when a goalkeeper makes a major mistake, it can lead to a goal and is often remembered for a long time. Some mistakes make people laugh and are shown regularly on TV.

Falling foul

Goalkeepers have to be careful not to foul an opponent who has the ball. If a goalkeeper makes a foul and is in his or her penalty area, the referee will give a penalty (see page 26). The referee may also send the goalkeeper off the pitch.

HALL OF FAME

Russian goalkeeper Lev Yashin let in a lot of goals in his first few games for Moscow Dynamo and was dropped from the team. But he worked hard and became a true legend. He is the only goalkeeper to win the prized European Player of the Year award. He is also believed to have saved more than 150 penalties during his career.

A goalkeeper fails to time his dive correctly and fouls Spain's Raul in the penalty area. The referee awarded a penalty kick.

Bouncing back

During a game goalkeepers try to put mistakes to the back of their minds. They have the rest of the match to concentrate on. After the game, they may watch their mistakes or talk to their coach. This helps goalkeepers solve problems in training.

Corners and free kicks

A corner kick is taken from a corner of the pitch. A free kick is awarded by the referee for a foul. Both offer a good chance for the attacking team to try and score a goal.

> " If you do not defend free kicks coming into your area from 45 yards out, you do not deserve to win. "
>
> – Sir Alex Ferguson, manager

A crowded area

During a corner or a wide free kick the penalty area can become crowded with players. Goalkeepers must make sure they have a clear view of the ball as it comes in. They also instruct their team-mates to mark opponents.

△ Satu Kunnas of Finland directs her defence. She points and shouts clear orders to her team-mates.

Corners and crosses

Many corners and free kicks are crossed high into the penalty area. Goalkeepers have to be strong and decisive if they go for the ball. They call for the ball to let their team-mates know they aim to catch it. If they cannot catch it, they can punch it.

▽ Zurab Mamaladze leaps to punch the ball clear from a corner kick.

> When you go for crosses, be loud. You have to let everybody know you're coming for it. A loud keeper gives defenders confidence.
>
> – Rachel Brown, England women's goalkeeper

Defensive wall

At free kicks, a goalkeeper may have to organise a defensive wall. This is a line of his or her team-mates who try to block the free kick. It is up to the goalkeeper to get the wall into the best position. The goalkeeper has to be ready in case a shot is curled over or around the defensive wall.

SKILLS TIPS

- Practise catching high balls at the top of your jump. Spread your hands around the back and sides of the ball.
- In training, get used to playing in goal behind a defensive wall.
- During a corner or free kick, do not get distracted. Keep your eye on the ball at all times.

Penalties

A penalty kick is given for a foul in the penalty area. It offers one team a very good chance to score, but the goalkeeper has a chance to make a great save.

> I think of penalty kicks as no-lose situations for a goalkeeper. All the pressure is on the outfield player, who is supposed to score.
>
> – Brad Friedel, USA goalkeeper

A guessing game

For a penalty kick the ball is placed on a spot just under 12 metres from the goal. Goalkeepers are allowed to move along their goal line before the ball is kicked. They try to guess where the ball will go and dive left or right, or stand tall if they think the ball will go down the middle.

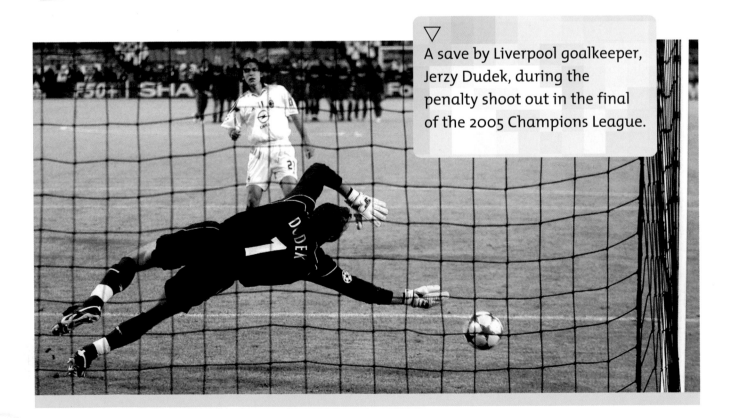

▽ A save by Liverpool goalkeeper, Jerzy Dudek, during the penalty shoot out in the final of the 2005 Champions League.

Penalty shoot outs

In some competitions, penalty shoot outs are used to decide the result of a drawn game. Teams take five penalties each, and if the scores are still drawn, more penalties are taken. The final of two World Cups, the 1994 men's and the 1999 women's, both went to shoot outs.

> Stay on your line and try to read which direction the kick is going to go. Remain upright as long as you can.
>
> – Peter Shilton, former England goalkeeper

▷ Brazil's goalkeeper, Dida, gets down quickly to make an important penalty save. He has deflected the ball around the goal post.

▷ HALL OF FAME

David Seaman played 75 times for England. He made two famous penalty saves at Euro 1996 and was picked as the keeper of the tournament.

Being the hero

Goalkeepers play a vital part in shoot outs. Their saves can be remembered for a long time. Portugal's goalkeeper, Ricardo, was the star of the shoot out between England and Portugal at Euro 2004. He saved a penalty and actually scored the winning penalty!

 Websites

http://www.progoalkeeper.co.uk
A great website dedicated to goalkeepers with lots of advanced coaching and fitness articles and tips.

http://www.goalkeepersaredifferent.com/homeground.htm
An interesting and unusual website looking at the lives and quirks of famous and not so famous keepers.

http://www.jbgoalkeeping.com/distribute.html
A very detailed guide to the skills of goalkeeping.

http://www.decatursports.com/drills/goalkeeping.htm
A long list of goalkeeping drills, exercises and practical tips from this US coaching website.

http://fifaworldcup.yahoo.com/o6/en
The official site of the 2006 World Cup held in Germany. It is packed with features and details of past and present World Cup tournaments.

http://www.uefa.com
The official website of UEFA, the organisation which runs football in Europe, including the Champions League.

http://www.ifhof.com/hof/halloffame.asp
Website of the International Football Hall of Fame where you can read long and detailed biographies of goalkeeping legends such as Dino Zoff, Gordon Banks and Lev Yashin.

http://www.edwinvandersar.com
The official website of Holland and Manchester United goalkeeping great, Edwin van der Sar.

http://www.francescotoldo.it/eng/index.htm
The official website of famous Italian goalkeeper, Francesco Toldo.

Every effort has been made by the Publishers to ensure that these websites contain no inappropriate or offensive material. However, because of the nature of the Internet, it is impossible to guarantee that the contents of these sites will not be altered. We strongly advise that Internet access is supervised by a responsible adult.

 Glossary

Clean sheet
– to not let in a goal throughout a whole game.

Clearance
– kicking or heading the ball out of defence.

Corner
– a kick taken from a corner of the pitch. It is given when the ball crosses the goal line of a defending team and one of their players was the last to touch it.

Cross
– sending the ball from the side of the pitch to the centre of the field, usually into the other team's penalty area.

Defensive wall
– a line of defenders standing close together to protect their goal against a free kick.

European Cup
– a competition played in by the best clubs in Europe. It is now known as the Champions League.

Flexibility
– being supple and able to bend easily.

Foul
– to break one of the rules of football.

Free kick
– how a team restarts the game after a foul.

Fumble
– to handle the ball poorly and lose control of it.

Goal kick
– a kick taken by the goalkeeper when an opposing player is the last one to touch the ball before it passes over your goal line.

Marking
– where a defender guards an opponent to try to stop him or her getting the ball.

Narrowing the angle
– when a goalkeeper moves towards an attacker to cut down how much of the goal the attacker can aim for.

One-on-one
– a situation where the attacker with the ball has just the goalkeeper to beat.

Opponent
– a player from the team you are playing against.

Penalty area
– a rectangular area in front of a goal inside which the goalkeeper can handle the ball.

Professional
– being paid a wage to play football.

Squad
– all the club's professional players, from which the manager chooses a team.

Stamina
– the ability to run and work hard for long periods.

World Cup
– a competition, held every four years, for the best national teams in the world.

Index

Out of My Comfort Zone

The Autobiography

Steve Waugh

MICHAEL JOSEPH
an imprint of
PENGUIN BOOKS

MICHAEL JOSEPH

Published by the Penguin Group

Penguin Books Ltd, 80 Strand, London WC2R 0RL, England

Penguin Group (USA) Inc., 375 Hudson Street, New York, New York 10014, USA

Penguin Group (Canada), 90 Eglinton Avenue East, Suite 700, Toronto, Ontario, Canada M4P 2Y3

(a division of Pearson Penguin Canada Inc.)

Penguin Ireland, 25 St Stephen's Green, Dublin 2, Ireland (a division of Penguin Books Ltd)

Penguin Group (Australia), 250 Camberwell Road,

Camberwell, Victoria 3124, Australia (a division of Pearson Australia Group Pty Ltd)

Penguin Books India Pvt Ltd, 11 Community Centre,

Panchsheel Park, New Delhi – 110 017, India

Penguin Group (NZ), cnr Airborne and Rosedale Roads, Albany,

Auckland 1310, New Zealand (a division of Pearson New Zealand Ltd)

Penguin Books (South Africa) (Pty) Ltd, 24 Sturdee Avenue,

Rosebank, Johannesburg 2196, South Africa

Penguin Books Ltd, Registered Offices: 80 Strand, London WC2R 0RL, England

www.penguin.com

First published in Australia by Penguin Books Australia 2005

First published in Great Britain By Michael Joseph 2006

1

Copyright © Steve Waugh, 2005

The moral right of the author has been asserted

All rights reserved

Without limiting the rights under copyright

reserved above, no part of this publication may be

reproduced, stored in or introduced into a retrieval system,

or transmitted, in any form or by any means (electronic, mechanical,

photocopying, recording or otherwise), without the prior

written permission of both the copyright owner and

the above publisher of this book

Set in 11.25/16 pt Garamond

Typeset by Post Pre-Press Group, Queensland, Australia

Printed in Australia by McPherson's Printing Group, Maryborough, Victoria

A CIP catalogue record for this book is available from the British Library

ISBN-13: 978–0–718–14833–1

ISBN-10: 0–718–14833–9

For my lifelong friend and partner, Lynette, who has endured and shared the best and worst times with me, whose nurturing ways, wisdom and unconditional love have comforted and inspired me.

And for our children, Rosalie, Austin and Lillian – you are life's most precious and greatest gifts. Your love of life, unique character and spirit make each and every day an adventure.

Of all my achievements, nothing matches the feeling of returning home to my family and the sight of you guys running up the hallway, trying to be the first to jump into my arms.